BURNT SAUSAGES
& PERFECT PIMM'S ®

Conceived, written and created by

CONTENTS

CONTENTS

FOREWORD BY JOHN TORODE

Despite the fact that I've lived in the UK for 14 years I'm a good Aussie boy at heart and barbies run through my blood as much as kangaroos, sunshine and cricket! I have very fond memories of quite literally 'slinging another snag on the barbie' back in Oz with lots of family and mates around but it was really an everyday happening; there is definitely something a little more eventful about barbecuing in the great British outdoors. Quite often invites go out long before our weathermen can possibly predict how wet the day could get, but this never seems to dampen enthusiasm. Shorts and flip-flops come out, salads prepared, meat marinated and of course, a huge jug of PIMM'S® is mixed up - quintessentially British with its mint, strawberries and cucumber.

There may be 'many ways to skin a cat' - there are even more to achieving BBQ nirvana. Some rely wholly on the carnivore diet; sausages, steaks, burgers, ribs and drumsticks, whilst others throw banana-leaf wrapped fish, veggie kebabs and whole peppers into the mix. I don't think there's much right or wrong in this; you can't complain when the guests bring their own food and normally compete to actually cook their meals themselves... sadly most seem to draw the line at doing the washing up!!

Outside cooking is nothing new; in fact if you think back it is the earliest from of cooking, big hunks of meat hanging over flames of fires that not only cooked but kept people warm during cold evenings (sounds familiar!?). Back in Australia my uncle Alex was BBQ king, he had it all down to a tee. He shopped for the BBQ meat and caught the fish, placing each strategically over the glowing coals from good wood, "Wood John, that's it, the secret," he would say. Now we're more likely to cook on coals which still give off that lovely waft of smoke - giving the food such distinctive flavours and a very evocative smell.

I am obviously passionate about food in general, but if I were to be on Mastermind, 'meat' would most definitely be my specialist subject. I continue to be amazed at the breadth and quality of meats available in this country. If I were to suggest a top five barbecue hit list for cuts of meat it would probably go as follows:

1.   Rump of Beef - great for steaks, fabulous marinated or threaded onto skewers
2.   Legs of Lamb - either slowly cooked whole with masses of garlic, or cut into steaks and served Greek style with lemon and parsley
3.   Wings and legs of chicken - chicken needs the skin to make it worth while, it really gives a great flavour

4. Pork loin on the bone - marinated Chinese style or just straight on as a big pork chop, the best finger food in the world
5. The great sausage! No barbie is a barbie without a barbecued snag wrapped in white bread and tomato sauce, lots of butter all dripping down the front of your shirt

Food and drink are not the only factors involved in a good BBQ, obviously creating an atmosphere and who you choose to share your meal with are just as important. There aren't many joys in life that can be shared with your most riotous mates or your granny and kids, a real crowd pleaser!

We have some fantastic cooking talent in this country, but even if you are no contender for Masterchef a barbie is the easy way to impress. Think about branching out with dishes such as a whole chicken filled with lemon and olives and cooked over the flames or even simply split the chicken down the centre and splash on some piri piri like they do in Portugal.

All in all it's a great way to relax, kick back and unwind; so enjoy this book, pull out some ideas, pour some PIMM'S® and have fun!

Happy Barbecuing,

John x

INTRODUCTION

SEAN HARGRAVE

There is a culinary revolution taking place on the lawns and patios of this island of ours; 75 million of them were held in this country last year and it's now twice as popular as the traditional Sunday roast during summer. This is the age of the great British BBQ.

Barbecuing is changing. No longer are the coals the preserve of an inexperienced dad burning bangers for long-suffering family and friends.

Today's barbecuer is more likely to have spent time preparing marinades and sourcing international recipes, to go with perfectly-cooked fish, lamb, or prime cuts of beef.

So, as those long, warm summer evenings finally descend upon us, it is time to do what people in the Caribbean and South America accidentally kick-started centuries ago, when they devised a means of cooking meat on wooden racks over coals burning in a trench.

The BBQ, you see, is not only becoming popular for great food, it is also stirring us into action to turn off the television, and get friends and family round for a great meal and an alfresco get-together.

We hope you delve into these pages and have fun finding out some curious facts about BBQs, and are inspired by the tasty recipes and great ideas for your next BBQ gathering.

Sean Hargrave
Editor

THE EVOLUTION OF THE BBQ...

1 Million BC ....Cavemen were not so different from today's BBQ fan - only without technology. Sticking bits of meat in an open fire was just plain cooking for them

850 BC ....Homer talks about the glee of roasting sausages over a fire in *The Odyssey*

64 ....Roman Emperor Nero's chef discovers a roasted pig's intestines are bloated. He decides to stuff the linings with meat and cooks them, so inventing the modern sausage

1066-1485 ....In the Middle Ages, huge feasts are prepared by spit-roasting carcasses on open fires. King Edward I's coronation in 1272 saw 278 bacon hogs, 450 pigs, 440 oxen, 430 sheep and 22,600 hens and chickens all barbecued

1200s ....Mongolian and Tartar warriors place meat under their saddle to tenderise it all day before it is cooked more speedily over a fire at night. The flattened meat is widely seen as the forerunner of the modern hamburger

1484 ....The forerunner of the hot dog sausage, the Frankfurter, is developed in Frankfurt

1600s ....Spanish explorers discover the last few remaining Taino Indians – a native South American tribe who could have been the first ever barbecuers. The Spanish learnt their 'barbacoa' form of cooking from the Taino Indians, which involved digging pits so their coals would be sheltered and cooking their food on wooden grills, and take the name home with them

Early 1800s ....New Yorkers were introduced to Hamburg Style Steaks, which were chopped up steaks made into patties that were then broiled. The recipe crossed the Atlantic with German settlers

1823 ....James Pimm opened his famous Oyster bar in the heart of London, where he developed the special blend of liqueurs and fruit extract that became known as PIMM'S® No 1 Cup – now seen by many Brits as the ultimate BBQ accompaniment

Late 1800s ....Cattle drives in America are believed to be the modern day derivation of the BBQ because cowboys were given brisket and found that if it were grilled for a long period over embers, rather than flames, it tasted a lot better

1880s ....German sausage seller, Antonoine Feuchtwanger, gets fed up of the expense of supplying customers with gloves to stop them burning their hands. His wife suggests he should make long, warmed rolls for them to go into. They called them 'Red Hots' but they soon became known as Hot Dogs

1904 ....A report in the New York Tribune credits 'Old Dave' of Athens, Texas with inventing the modern hamburger in a bun which he sells at the St Louis World's Fair

1907 ....Scott Paper Co. introduced the first paper towel serviette

1920 ....Henry Ford invented charcoal briquettes

1934 ....A restaurant in Louisville, Kentucky claims to have served the first cheeseburger

1951 . . . . .The modern BBQ is born when George Stephens, an employee at Weber Brothers steelworks near Chicago, sees that by chopping a buoy in half and using the bottom half for coals and the top half as a lid he can control home BBQs much better without worrying about wind and mess

1951 . . . . .Tupperware introduced

1985 . . . . .First gas grill introduced claiming to offer full flavour with none of the mess of charcoal

TEN THINGS YOU NEVER KNEW ABOUT SAUSAGES

1 . . . . The term 'sausage' comes from the Latin for 'something salted'.

2 . . . . Sausages first became known as 'bangers' during WW2 because excess water added made them explode in the frying pan.

3 . . . . Homer wrote about them in *The Odyssey* more than 2,800 years ago.

4 . . . . Queen Victoria was a huge fan, but liked her meat chopped rather than minced.

5 . . . . There are more than 400 varieties of sausage to choose from.

6 . . . . Sausages are bought in nine out of ten UK households.

7 . . . . They're served at 70% of BBQs, making them the most common BBQ food.

8 . . . . The most popular day for eating sausages is Saturday.

9 . . . . The UK spends almost half a billion pounds on sausages every year.

10 . . . . Those in the know agree that you should never prick a sausage - as it lets the flavour out.

COUNTING CALORIES

Whilst sausages are never going to be a dieter's dream food, there is some good news for health-conscious BBQ fans. A Food Standards Agency survey in 2003 revealed that the humble BBQ is the healthiest way of cooking a banger.

So, whilst it's not a green light to gorge, at least you can rest assured that with a BBQ you get the full taste of an unpricked sausage without the extra calories or fat.

Cooking method	Calories (per 100g)	Fat (g per 100g)
Grilled (unpricked)	306	19.9
Grilled (pricked)	284	18.9
Fried	285	20.8
Baked	298	19.9
Barbecued	292	18.1

NO MORE BURNT BANGERS

If you're fed up with being served burnt bangers - and let's face it, who hasn't been offered what would pass for a charred cigar in many quarters? – remember there are ways to prevent this.

One solution is to poach sausages before you put them on the grill. Just leave the sausages simmering in water for twenty to thirty minutes and they'll be mainly cooked, but look a bit pasty. Five or ten minutes on the BBQ grill will brown them off and leave you with evenly cooked bangers with a crisp coating and smoky flavour.

Poaching sausages will also protect your sausage skins from bursting in the intense heat of a BBQ, which can also cook the meat too quickly and unevenly.

Sausage Envy

BBQs AROUND THE WORLD

Whilst Brits are only unique in their insistence at wearing bad taste aprons and barbecuing at the first sign of sunshine, our friends around the globe have far more exceptional ways of interpreting the joy of the BBQ.

Japan is unique in having a tradition of bars, called Yakitoriya, which are built around BBQ grills (yes, sounds perfect to us too – why have these not yet caught on in Britain?) The term comes from the skewers of succulent chicken, dipped in BBQ sauce that are most often served here, called Yakitori. Yaki means grilled and Tori means chicken. The professional classes, in particular, like nothing better than leaving the office after a hard day and having a drink with their skewer of barbecued chicken. And the Japanese don't waste anything when it comes to the chicken – your skewer could contain: momo yaki (legs); hatsu yaki (hearts); kawa yaki (skin); or bonchiri yaki ('pope's noses') to name but a few. Other popular foods you may find on your skewers at Yakitoriya, include shitake mushrooms, gingko nuts and quail eggs. The Japanese do still throw BBQs in their own gardens, just as the British do. The main thing to remember here is not to point your chopsticks at anyone, it is seen as rude; and if you are offered grilled eel, be very thankful to your host, it is a great honour.

South Africa is unusual as it is an (at least partly) English speaking country but uses a word that doesn't even sound like BBQ. The braai (pronounced bri) is an institution in a country whose weather encourages outdoor eating. Like BBQ the word "braai" refers to the grill itself and can also be used as a verb "to braai some steak" or hold a "braai". Typical dishes include biltong - dried meat strips (often from game or ostrich); boerewors - spicy sausages; and sosaties - spicy marinated mutton skewers.

America has enjoyed a long-term love affair with al fresco cooking. Three in four households own a BBQ and the majority use them year round, at least five times a month, making the country easily the most BBQ mad in the world. While the food remains similar to the UK, the main difference is a near even split between men and women cooking at the grill. Barbecuing is particularly popular in the Southern states of the USA not only because of good weather, but also history. From the 1800s onwards, European settlers raised pigs, which were allowed to forage in nearby woods. When the village supply of pork ran low, local men would go hunting and come back with pigs that would be communally cooked on a large BBQ.

"Did you know the Australians have 59 words for 'barbecue'?"

Australia has the great weather and laid back attitude that has forever linked their cuisine with a 'barbie'. For the Aussies this is not just an excuse for an outdoor party but a way of life. A huge variety of familiar meat, but more seafood than in Britain, is served up at an Aussie 'barbie'. Barbecuers down under have also long held a secret of ensuring their steaks hold in a unique flavour – they brush lager on them!

In **New Zealand**, the Maori 'Hangi' may also have been a forerunner to the BBQ. Kiwis, like their Southern hemisphere neighbours, see barbecuing as a way of life but nowadays few would go the effort required to prepare a 'Hangi'. A Hangi is an age-old traditional Maori/Polynesian-style banquet of meat and root vegetables all cooked in a hole dug deep in the ground. Special stones are heated in a fire and placed in the earthen pit, with baskets of food put on top before having earth piled over and left for several hours – hope they have plenty of garlic bread and dips to start!

The **Caribbean** is also arguably the birth place of the BBQ, so no surprise that the great weather and miles of beaches makes the string of islands, the perfect place to slice open an oil drum (don't try that at home!) and cook locally caught fish and spicy cuts of chicken and pork in the bottom half, with the top half providing a lid.

BBQ NAME GAMES

Spain is not only synonymous with grilling fresh fish on the beach or stirring a frying pan of paella on an open BBQ, it has a very good claim to naming the cooking genre. Its early explorers in South America came across the Taino Indians (arguably the first barbecuers) and returned to Europe with the word 'barbacoa' - their best take on what the natives called their style of cooking fish over a pit of coals.

France not only has a love of grilling food outdoors, its language is another contender for naming the BBQ and has various cases to prove it. The phrase 'barbe a queue' means 'whiskers to tail' or 'de la barbe a la queue' means 'from the beard to the tail'. Infinitely preferable (we're not sure about eating anything with a beard) is the French 'barbaque', meaning roast mutton.

Romania provides yet another contender for naming the BBQ. The dish most likely go be put on a grill (since the Middle Ages) in the East European country is mutton, which is called 'barbec'.

WORST EVER BBQ

The accolade for worst BBQ ever must surely go to a group of soldiers from an undisclosed army.*

Finding a discarded tank that had obviously come off second best in an exchange of fire, they decided to use its turret for an impromptu BBQ. After lighting a fire just underneath the turret hole they assembled the day's rations and looked forward to a feast.

Unfortunately, they were soon to find out how naked flames and ammunition are not the most congenial BBQ guests. After a few sparks from the fire set off a larger fire inside the tank, the soldiers heard a suspicious 'fizzing' sound. To be safe, and with good reason, they ran for cover.

The tank immediately exploded, full, as it was, with ammunition that had not yet been salvaged. The explosion flattened their camp, although mercifully nobody was injured, and the tank's turret was blown a considerable distance into a nearby river where the rations that had been lined up for cooking floated away.

* Details have been removed to protect the ignorant!

═ A RIGHT ROYAL BARBECUE, BY JENNIE BOND ═

As the BBC's Royal Correspondent, we've seen Jennie Bond at all of the big royal occasions in the last fifteen years. A journalist and mother, Jennie also appeared on our screens in 2003 sampling the great outdoors in "I'm a celebrity... Get me out of here."

"It is the perfect summer event. The very word 'barbecue' invokes visions of peace and tranquillity, sunshine and relaxation, good food and a glass of something special. PIMM'S® would do nicely, thank you.

There's something delightfully informal about barbecues. You never need to ask whether it's smart or casual. You know as soon as you're invited that it's a shorts and T-shirt occasion. Everyone will wander around helping - or interfering - with the cooking, and you don't have to worry about setting the table: this is the great outdoors... people are happy to eat standing up, sitting on the ground or perched on a stool.

Even the royals enjoy a barbecue - though they tend to call it a 'picnic' and they do have a proper table and chairs. Prince Philip has a well-earned reputation as head chef when they're eating al fresco - mind you, he has the ultimate luxury of everything being prepared for him in advance. His job is simply to pop the steaks and sausages, chicken or venison on the barbie and cook them to perfection, and he's said to be a dab hand at it.

A favourite location for royal barbecues is one of the cabins dotted around the Balmoral estate in Scotland. The Queen and many of her family spend up to ten weeks there every summer. From the Castle, they set off either on foot or in a Land Rover – often with the Queen at the wheel – and meet up at a cabin on the banks of the River Dee.

One of the Queen's cousins told me that the royal party once arrived to find a couple of hikers enjoying the comfort of the cabin. They discussed shooing them away but the Queen Mother had quite a different plan: she got out of the car and invited the hikers to stay for lunch. Which they did – and have no doubt dined out on the story ever since!

Although the basic preparation of the food is generally done for them, the royals don't mind getting their hands dirty....well, wet, at least. While Prince Philip tends to the barbecue, the Queen has been known to rustle up a salad dressing – and she can be quite insistent about doing the washing-up.

Barbecues really are a bit of a 'happening'. You're never quite sure how it's all going to turn out and there's something rather comforting about the way everyone joins in.

As a reporter, I remember covering the Labour Party campaign during the General Election of 1992. Almost to the final day the pundits were saying that Neil Kinnock was on course to win. When it all went horribly wrong I had to stand outside his London home – along with a crowd of other hacks – hoping for a word with the poor man. Needless to say, Mr Kinnock ignored us and sought solace instead in the bosom of his family. And how did they try to raise his spirits? Well, at about 7pm, the unmistakable aroma of a barbecue wafted across the road from the Kinnocks' back garden. Sorted!

These days I'm lucky enough to live by the sea in Devon. As we sit with our neighbours sipping our drinks, with the barbecue sizzling and the boats bobbing by, I sometimes think life couldn't possibly get any better.

But then it does. A friend will ring and suggest an impromptu fishing trip. We meet on the beach as the sun heads towards the horizon and hope that the mackerel are passing by. With any luck, they are – and we cast out our lines. The children, oblivious of chilly British waters, take an evening dip while we dig a hole in the sand.

We cheer and holler as the first fish is landed: it's the signal to line the hole with firewood and prepare for a feast. The children find some slates along the beach and put them on the burning embers: in no time at all, the barbecue is all fired up and ready to go.

Nothing tastes better than freshly caught mackerel with some sweet potatoes (wrapped in foil and cooked on the stones) and some of my husband's home-grown yellow courgettes (halved, smothered in olive oil and browned on the barbie).

It may not be Australia; we may well be sitting on the beach cloaked in fleeces and rugs – but a barbecue by the sea on a summer's evening in Britain with a PIMM'S® by my side really is my idea of paradise."

Jennie Bond

TOP BBQ FILM MOMENTS

- The Beans BBQ scene from 'Blazing Saddles'
- The Wilkes' grand BBQ in 'Gone with the Wind' where Scarlett first encounters Rhett Butler
- Johnny Depp flipping burgers in 'Edward Scissorhands'
- Jerry Maguire's wedding BBQ with Cuba Gooding Jr singing
- In 'Father of the Bride', George's stress about his daughter's wedding culminates in his tearing packs of hot dog and burger rolls to shreds before the family BBQ
- Cynthia's BBQ in 'Secrets and Lies' where she reveals the true identity of her guest Hortense
- Nick's BBQ in 'Pushing Tin' where Russell humiliates Nick on the basketball court
- 'National Lampoons European Vacation' where Clark Griswold's BBQ pit explodes

"Eating is not merely a material pleasure. Eating well gives a spectacular joy to life and contributes immensely to goodwill and happy companionship. It is of great importance to the morale."

ELSA SCHIAPARELLI

"A perfect summer day is when the sun is shining, the breeze is blowing, the birds are singing, and the lawn mower is broken."

JAMES DENT

BBQ TIPS FROM CELEBRITY CHEF, JOHN TORODE

Celebrity chef and presenter of BBC's Masterchef Goes Large: John Torode also runs the renowned Smiths of Smithfield restaurant in London. As an Australian, John's ideally placed to give advice on BBQ recipes.

'It's summer and time for a BBQ and glass of PIMM'S®!

Being an Aussie and also being passionate about good meat – and food in general – I get very excited about lighting the first barbie of the year. Now I'm settled in England, I've accepted that it's just as likely to be under a rain umbrella rather than a sun shade but that rarely puts me off! Here are a few of my top tips should you happen to have a few mates coming over for a big BBQ:

Warm the oven, things like the sausages can always be cooked up first and kept warm. If everyone's ready to get stuck in just dish up in fresh white bread with Tommy Sauce as the starter.

Cook with larger pieces of meat first, ahead of the more obvious burgers/ sausages/ chicken pieces; the bigger cuts of meat will hold heat while you continue to cook the rest of your food.

Buy a great BBQ with multi-layers, so as things are nearly cooked they can be moved away from the heat, so they don't dry out and over cook.

Everyone likes BBQ sausages and now that you can get such great vegetarian ones have these on standby as an option for any veggies.

Last, but not least, have a couple of large jugs of PIMM'S® made up with all the bits to get the party going. Fill the cool-box with ice and let your friends drop their drink in to use as a communal fridge, tie a cork screw and bottle opener to the fence and enjoy the sunshine."

JOHN TORODE'S
BASHED OUT CHICKEN WITH LEMON AND GARLIC GREEK STYLE
SERVES 10 WITH A COUPLE OF EXTRAS

The secret to great cooking is fresh quality ingredients. A good chicken will not shrink very much when you cook it, so make sure you buy quality. The Greeks are clever cooks who use lesser cuts of meat for flavour but also marinate them to tenderise. This recipe is a prime example of the clever cooking they do. A civilisation as old as the Greeks can't be wrong.

12 chicken thighs with the bones removed
10 cloves of Garlic
1 tsp of salt (preferably flaked)
2 lemons, juiced
200mls olive oil
A large handful, oregano or marjoram
(yes fresh!)

A large handful, flat leaf parsley
200g black pitted olives
100g plum tomatoes
200g crumbled feta cheese

Take the chicken and using a sharp knife, score the skin, lay the boned thighs out flat in a large dish ready to marinade. Crush the garlic and mix with the salt, 100mls of olive oil and all the lemon juice. Rub the chicken well and leave for an hour or so.

In a food processor blend the parsley and marjoram with the remaining olive oil. Pour half this mix over the chicken and give it a good stir around.

Cut the tomatoes into little chunks about the size of a dice and mix with the olives and the remaining green olive oil mix.

Place the marinated chicken over hot coals and give them a good blast of heat, then turn after 2 minutes, lift them a little higher away from the heat and cook for 15 minutes, or so, turning often.

Take from the heat and place in a large flat serving dish, drizzle with the olive and tomato mix and then sprinkle over the crumbled feta cheese.

Serve.

"I'm a man. Men cook outside. Women make the three-bean salad. That's the way it is and always has been, since the first settlers of Levittown. That outdoor grilling is a manly pursuit has long been beyond question. If this wasn't firmly understood, you'd never get grown men to put on those aprons with pictures of dancing wienies and things on the front..."

WILLIAM GEIST

PUBLIC BBQS

One of the great pleasures of the summer can be visiting Britain's beautiful outdoor spaces and enjoying a BBQ with friends – perhaps after a ramble, or fishing trip, but it can be something of a minefield working out where you can, and where you can't, hold BBQs.

The Country Code, even after revision in 2004, surprisingly does not mention BBQs – although it does mention people should not endanger flowers or wildlife. A spokesman for The Countryside Agency can only say that in the absence of specific advice that, "people need to be aware of the dangers of lighting a BBQ and not light them willy nilly". However, the agency does offer the positive advice that if any area calls itself a Country Park, then it quite often has a designated BBQ area.

The National Trust lists a handful of sites that have dedicated BBQ facilities or encourage people to bring their own equipment for an al fresco family meal. They include:

Gumber Bothy, near Arundel, West Sussex
Clumber Park, near Worksop
Studland Beach and Nature Reserve, near Swanage, Dorset

Other local authority attractions with gardens and beautiful scenery, which readily market themselves to barbecuers include:

Fort Victoria beach on the Isle of Wight
Hayling Island in Hampshire

With a new right to roam law opening up more land for public enjoyment, coinciding with a huge rise in people timing BBQs to coincide with outdoor pursuits, clearly there is a need for further guidance for 'out and about' barbecuers. Until there is, here is our top advice...

TOP ADVICE TO
'OUT AND ABOUT' BARBECUERS:

. . . . . To find out whether you can hold your BBQ in a particular public space, contact the national park, land owner or local authority that you wish to hold a BBQ in. For National Parks, also log on to www.nationalparks.gov.uk

. . . . . Always respect the environment that you're holding your BBQ in, as well as the people around you and tidy up the area after you've finished

. . . . . Bear in mind the potential dangers of lighting a BBQ and remain responsible at all times

. . . . . If you're unsure about where you can BBQ, why not take part in a general public BBQ – keep an eye out in your local press for details of BBQs that you'll be able to join

MOST EXTREME

For most people a leisurely stroll is all that's needed to build up an appetite for a BBQ. For a group of extreme sports enthusiasts in New Zealand, however, that seemed far too mundane. Instead they came up with the novel idea of cooking as they bungee jumped.

A raft with a BBQ grill was placed on Waiapoa Lake and then each adrenalin-junkie jumped the 250ft drop with burger and fork in hand. The idea was to cook each burger as they bobbed up and down - a cooking method that took one and a half hours per burger.

WHY BURN WOOD TWICE?

With a back garden surrounded by trees it may seem bizarre that instead of lopping off a few branches and throwing them on the fire, most BBQs start with a trip to the local garage to buy a bag of charcoal. However, as odd as it may seem, there is a very good reason for buying burnt wood, and then burning it again...

Wood is packed with water as well as toxic gases that can turn food carcinogenic – the process for creating charcoal involves burning off these gases such as hydrogen and methane, as well as the more dangerous benzopyrene – meaning that chefs can cook outdoors without covering the family's bangers in poisonous sooty deposits.

The secret with producing charcoal lies in burning wood in a vacuum, normally a huge air-tight container, or sometimes underground. The vacuum allows the heat of the fire to dry out the wood quickly – the equivalent would be leaving a log in the shed for a year – and also allows for the poisonous gases to combust.

In order for carbon to burn, it needs oxygen, which is why the process takes place in a vacuum - where no oxygen is present. The original wood is burnt down to around a quarter of its original size, however all of the carbon remains - leaving you with carbon-rich charcoal as we know it.

WHITE FOR READY

Lime is more normally used in mortar for building houses, but when added to charcoal it serves the very useful task of glowing white to indicate to the chef when it's ready to cook.

The lime is added when charcoal is turned into briquettes – the process by which rough pieces of charred wood are turned into more aesthetically pleasing rounded, uniform lumps. The briquettes also have nitrate added, to help with lighting, and borax to gel them together.

HOME GROWN?

In the UK we burn around 45,000 tonnes of charcoal every year, yet only 5,000 tonnes comes from British forests; instead, most of the charcoal thrown onto a BBQ is likely to have travelled in excess of 12,000 miles from South Africa, Brazil or Nigeria.

Environmentalists point out that in London alone we throw away more than 50,000 tonnes of tree waste every year – that's not only enough to heat 20,000 homes through the winter, it's easily enough to provide charcoal for all of the city's BBQs in the summer.

"Cook with it? Oh no, it was far too expensive for that"

PERFECT PIMM'S®

The onset of the British summer is inextricably linked with the great British tradition of PIMM'S® and lemonade. PIMM'S® No.1 Cup, is seen by many as the quintessential British summertime drink and is therefore the perfect compliment to your great British BBQ.

PIMM'S® spirit drink was created in the 1840s, by the owner of a popular Oyster Bar in the City of London - James Pimm, originally a shellfish monger. Pimm offered the spirit - a gin-based drink containing a secret mixture of liqueurs, fruit extracts and herbs, as an aid to digestion, and served it in a small tankard. The reaction of his city gentlemen clientele was instant and enthusiastic. The spirit drink was for many years served by the pint and this is where the 'No. 1 Cup', with reference to the tankards, arose.

By the 1870s, business was booming and a chain of five PIMM'S® spirit drink restaurants were set up across the City of London. By the late 1920s, PIMM'S® was being exported all over the world.

In later years, PIMM'S® extended their range from the original No. 1, No. 2 (based on whisky) and No. 3 Cup (brandy) invented by James Pimm. A number of other spirits were used as bases for new 'Cups': No. 4 employed rum, No. 5 rye and No. 6 vodka. PIMM'S® is nowadays the number one British summertime drink and is very much part of the English summer season – seen everywhere from Wimbledon and Ascot to our garden BBQs.

HOW TO SERVE THE PERFECT PIMM'S®

Take a tall chilled glass, pint or jug and fill to two thirds with ice. Mix one part PIMM'S® to three parts quality lemonade, and stir gently. The final key is garnish. Top up with slices of orange and lemon to bring a nice summery zing, adding slices of cucumber and a sprig of mint for the essential coolness.

If even that is too much effort on a lazy summer day, PIMM'S® can now be purchased in ready-to-drink cans and bottles.

The PIMM'S, PIMM'S No.1 and No.1 CUP words and numeral are trade marks.   **DRINKAWARE.CO.UK**

JOHN TORODE'S
AVOCADO, BACON AND SPINACH SALAD WITH CREAMY DRESSING

A good staple salad is important to any BBQ, I have a couple that I like to do when friends come over but this is my champion. There is something cooling about avocado and I am a sucker for a creamy dressing!

You will need a heavy based frying pan and a slotted kitchen spoon, two medium sized bowls, and a whisk or electric beater.

100g pancetta, cut into lardons
100ml vegetable oil
2 thick slices white bread or half a baguette
40g grated Parmesan
2 Avocados
300g young leaf spinach
40g shaved Parmesan
Freshly ground black pepper

In a heavy based frying pan heat 100ml vegetable oil and add the lardons. Fry gently over a medium heat moving constantly so that they don't stick or burn. When crisp remove from the pan with a slotted spoon and drain well on kitchen paper.

Cut the bread into 1cm cubes and place in the oil in which the bacon was fried, and cook for a few minutes. Turn when lightly coloured, and continue to cook until all sides are well coloured. Remove from the oil with a slotted spoon and drain on kitchen paper. Whilst they are still warm, place in a bowl and sprinkle over the 40g of grated Parmesan.

Cut the avocado from the top until you hit the seed and then run the knife all the way around the seed so the avocado looks like it is cut through. Twist the bottom anti-clockwise and the top clockwise and pull apart. The seed should be left in the centre of one side.

Hold the half with the seed in your left hand (the right if you are left handed) and with a medium size knife gently strike the seed, the knife should stick into the seed, twist the knife in an anti-clockwise direction and release the seed. Take a kitchen spoon and push it down one side between the flesh and the skin and run it all the way around to remove the flesh. Repeat with remaining avocados. Slice each half into four even pieces from top to bottom.

Wash the spinach and set to one side in a large bowl.

The Dressing
I medium egg
I egg yolk
I tbsp Dijon mustard
I tbsp shallot vinegar
I garlic clove, crushed
200ml vegetable oil
200ml olive oil
I75g freshly grated Parmesan

Whisk the egg, egg yolk, mustard, vinegar and garlic in a large bowl until the mixture begins to thicken and turn pale. Slowly add the oils, whisking constantly, until well amalgamated – add a little hot water if the mixture seems too thick. Then stir in 150g grated Parmesan.

Place the avocado and spinach in a large serving bowl, scatter with the croutons and lardons, finish with the remaining shaved Parmesan and a grinding of black pepper. Pour over a good amount of dressing and serve.

"*An onion can make people cry,
but there has never been a vegetable invented to make them laugh.*"

WILL ROGERS

"*I am not a vegetarian because I love animals;
I am a vegetarian because I hate plants.*"

A. WHITNEY BROWN

"*Summer afternoon, summer afternoon; to me those have always been
the two most beautiful words in the English language*"

JAMES DENT

FEEDING THE 5,000...
AND 39,000 OF THEIR FRIENDS

If you ever worry about having enough food to make sure all your guests are content, spare a thought for organisers at Sydney's Warwick Farm racecourse who held the world's largest BBQ in 1993. To set a Guinness World Record they fed 44,158 guests 300,000 sausages, 100,000 steaks and 50,000 chicken burgers. On average, each guest ate 6.8 sausages, 2.26 steaks and 1.13 chicken burgers.

A SMOKING IDEA

"Fish is held out to be one of the greatest luxuries of the table and not only necessary, but even indispensable at all dinners where there is any pretence of excellence or fashion."

ISABELLA BEETON

Although he is passionate about his smoked fish, Patrick Wilkins of Swallow Fish in Northumberland (www.swallowfish.co.uk) admits that the smell of kippers cooking in the kitchen is not for everyone.

Hence, he reasons, it's why they're one of his best sellers during the BBQ season: "They taste great to me all year round but a lot of people don't like the house to smell, so they start buying as soon as it's time for a BBQ because the aroma doesn't hang around in the garden."

Patrick's other firm favourite for the BBQ is smoked salmon steaks which, like kippers, he suggests people put straight above the grill as close as possible to the charcoal, so that the coals can add a little more to the smoked flavour. In many ways this is simply repeating the smoking process but at a higher temperature.

For other fish, such as sea bass, sardines, salmon fillets and scallops he suggests stuffing the fish with a little butter and couple of pinches of your favourite herbs, plus a generous squeeze of lemon juice.
"Then as the fish cooks, the herbs all get into the flesh of the meat, and the juices

steam it so it's really tender and tastes great," he enthuses.

For the more 'meaty' fish he suggests kebabs. The trick is to pick fish that are roughly the same thickness, so each chunk cooks at the same speed.

Patrick continues, "My favourite is to marinade the fish briefly in a sauce and then put the chunks of salmon, monk fish and king prawns still in their shells on skewer spaced out with pepper slices," he adds.

As Patrick has proved, fish is not only healthy and great at adding a touch of class to any BBQ, but very easy too - it is no wonder it is rapidly gaining popularity a British BBQs.

"In the hands of an able cook,
fish can become
an inexhaustible source
of perpetual delight."

JEAN-ANTHELME BRILLAT-SAVARIN

GOING THE EXTRA MILE

Most BBQ cooks can only dream of having a grill wider than a couple of plates but the residents of Karadeniz Eregil in Turkey quite literally went the extra mile to make sur their 2002 Anchovy Festival would never be forgotten.

The 1,600 metre (5,294ft) long BBQ set a world record for the widest ever BBQ gril and would've taken an Olympic athlete about four minutes to run from one end to the other.

Canada claims the record of having the longest ever BBQ - stretching from one side o the vast country to the other. Thousands took part in a massive, simultaneous outdoc celebration on Canada Day in August 2003, for an event to support Canadian Bee Farmers.

"Excellent in-flight catering - but the bar's not so convenient"

THE WEATHER

Whether the weather be hot,
or whether the weather be not,
We'll weather the weather,
whatever the weather,
Whether we like it or not!

It's typical, the one thing that we can never control when it comes to BBQs is probably the single most important factor in holding one – namely the weather.

The unpredictable nature of the great British weather may also help to explain the propensity and popularity of BBQs in this country. As soon as we see the merest hint of sun peeping through the clouds, we all rush outside to dust off our BBQs, send someone down the supermarket to stock up and hit the phones in the competitive rush to be the first with the great idea – thus making sure that all your friends have to come to your BBQ. All the time, we're driven by that nagging, undeniable fear - that we really never know when we'll next get the chance.

Spontaneous BBQs, hastily arranged as soon as the mercury starts to rise are all well and good, but what if you want to plan yours in advance to make sure that you're thoroughly prepared? If you're really house-proud, you'll want the time to make sure your home and garden are both looking their absolute best to show off to the neighbours. What's more, if you want to be sure to get all of your busy friends along, you're going to have to invite them well in advance to get a slot in their jam-packed social diaries.

PREDICTING THE WEATHER

Planning a BBQ in advance though, is fraught with the danger that's inherent in predicting the weather. Whilst this has never been an exact science, there are many different ways – some more scientific than others - of trying to second-guess the temperamental British summertime:

THE GOOD OLD WEATHER FORECAST

Most weather forecasting websites such as www.weather.co.uk, or the BBC weather forecast offer long-term forecasts, but be aware, most judges maintain that it's almost impossible to accurately predict the weather more than five days in advance. Or check out www.anyoneforpimms.com where you'll find a BBQ weather predictor throughout the summer.

TRUST IN NATURE

There are all manners of old wives' tales when it comes to predicting the weather – some of them with more basis in science than others. Take your pick from these: Hang seaweed outside your front door; if the seaweed stays damp chances are you'll be in for rain. Pinecones are another favourite – a pinecone will open out if you're in for dry weather, and close up if it's going to rain. And if you happen to live near a field of cows, keep an eye on their posture – if they're lying down, it's not because they're lazy, but because they think rain is on the way.

LOCAL KNOWLEDGE

Guaranteed there will be a local weather forecasting expert in your area with decades' worth of statistics all stacked up with the sole purpose of proving themselves more accurate than the professionals – scour your local newspaper for details and follow their advice closely.

Following the law of averages you can also predict which weeks are likely to be the best to hold a BBQ. June gets the most hours of sunlight, but may be a little cooler than July and August.

Month	Hours of sunlight	Ave temp min °C	Ave temp max °C	Average rainfall (mm)
May	6	8	17	46
June	7	12	20	45
July	6	14	22	57
August	6	13	21	59
Sept	5	11	19	49

WHAT TO DO IF IT RAINS?

Rest assured if it does rain at your BBQ, however, it's not the end of the world. Follow these steps to make the best of the situation.

There will always be at least one hardy soul who'll cheerily insist on continuing to BBQ outside, on his own, in the rain, in the view that "it's just a passing shower". Rule number one is – let them. You can retire indoors and wait in the dry until your food is ready and can be brought in to you.

- Have a sheltered section in your garden to site the BBQ - but never BBQ in a shed or garage!
- Keep several large golf umbrellas on stand by, just in case the rain hits and you still need to get out and about in the garden
- Keep the window open to catch all of those authentic BBQ smells
- Enjoy a refreshing glass of PIMM'S®, with fruit and mint – it tastes just as good when you're indoors
- Have a selection of music on hand just in case you need to keep people amused – as the host, guests will be looking to you to entertain them

"Nothing like eating al fresco, is there darling?"

SAUSAGE 'CHAMPION OF CHAMPIONS'

If there is one meat David Lishman is passionate about it's pork. This is because the owner of Lishmans Butcher in Ilkley in Yorkshire is a firm believer that the only way to make award-winning sausages is with the best ingredients.

He should know. He's scoured his area to track down rare pig breeders to ensure that the pork he sells as cuts of meat or as sausages are worthy of the prestigious 'National Sausage Champion of Champions' title he has won twice.

"Sausages are like anything, you only get out what you've put in," he insists. "There's nothing wrong with the farmers that breed pigs in intensive units, they're producing affordable meat for the mass market. I specialise in rare breed pigs that are far tastier because they're allowed to take longer to mature, and so they have a better flavour, and the meat only costs around 10-15% extra."

David favours Saddleback, Gloucester Old Spot, Tamworth and British lop breeds, which are ready for market at 26-28 weeks compared to the 16-18 weeks average.

"It means they've got extra time to develop fat and to mature so they're far more succulent," David explains.

"The problem with some modern meat is it's made to be far too lean because people think it's healthy, but that just means that it's tasteless. There are three important factors for sausages; succulence, flavour and tenderness. To my mind, you only get all three if you stick with the old breeds that are farmed free range."

By allowing pigs to roam naturally, rather than being confined to a pen, David believes the final flavour is far more natural. The rationale for this is that the animals are natural foragers who love to snack on grass, herbage and roots in a field as well as purpose-made feed.

Being outside they also get to exercise and enjoy the outdoors, which is crucial from an animal welfare point of view because pigs are widely regarded as the cleanest and most intelligent animal on the farm. By sourcing his meat carefully, David feels confident the pigs have been reared in the best possible circumstances and so the meat is as succulent, tasty and tender as possible.

The cuts of meat that go into a sausage are vitally important because the balance between meat and fat has to be just right. Hence, David only ever uses meat from the shoulder and belly in equal measure because this not only makes the final sausage succulent; it also ensures it is moist.

David's top award-winning sausage recipes are mainly secret, although he is mor
than willing to give those starting out with making their own sausages some tip
and starter recipes.

As a rule of thumb, he suggests that a sausage should be at least 70% ground por
meat and whatever weight you start off with, always make sure around 2%
seasoning, mainly salt and pepper. The rest needs to be breadcrumbs (referred t
as rusk) preferably from white bread.

"Rusk can sometimes be looked down on because some people use it to make
cheap product by using too much and bulking it out with too much water," he say

"It's a vital ingredient of a British sausage and gives it a lighter texture. In the res
of Europe they tend to not use rusk and it gives a far heavier, solid sausage. There
nothing wrong with that, it's just not to the traditional British taste."

In addition to salt and pepper as seasoning, David often uses nutmeg, mace an
chives which can also be added to make up the 2% (estimated) proportion o
seasoning.

"Hi honey, I'm homo sapiens"

THE CHAMPION OF CHAMPIONS ON THE BBQ

Like many of us, if the sun's shining on Yorkshire on a Sunday, there's nothing David likes more than barbecuing some of his renowned sausages for friends and family. Whilst some of his recipes are closely guarded, here is a guide to making the type of sausages he would normally make at home for the BBQ. Typically, he would chose meat from his favourite breeds, the Saddleback or British lop.

2kg of pork (half of boneless shoulder and half belly pork)
10g ground white pepper
Handful of chopped sage
Splash of cold water

40g salt
Pinch ground nutmeg
200g breadcrumbs (white bread)

"You just mix the ingredients to the minced pork for a couple of minutes until it's well mixed but still moist," explains David.

"That's where the splash of cold water comes in. You need to keep the mixture moist to ensure the breadcrumbs are hydrated."

After a couple of minutes the mixture should be right. David cannot give an example of what the consistency should be similar to but assures it is something that with experience 'you get a feel for'. Then it's a case of getting the mixture into the membranes.

"That's the fun part," he jokes. "I've used a funnel and spoon in the past, but it can be a bit tricky so if you expect to keep on making sausages at home it's probably best to buy a little machine, they're not too expensive."

After going to all that effort it would be an affront to the rare breed pigs to offer guests burnt bangers, so David is vigilant until the end.

"If you're using coals, you've got to make sure they're white and not still smoking or flaming," he warns.

"If you put the sausages on too early you'll just find the outsides cook too soon and get burnt. That's why I now always use a good quality gas grill because it's controllable and has a lid you can shut to seal in the smoke and flavour."

All you then need to do is turn the sausages regularly to ensure they cook evenly. When they're cooked all the way through, serve to guests, who David assures, will be able to taste the difference.

WHY 'HAM' WHEN THEY'RE MADE OF BEEF?

When German immigrants settled in New York in the early 19th century they will have had no way of knowing that when they brought over a recipe for minced, broiled steaks, they were paving the way for the food revolution that became known as the hamburger.

The original recipe came from Hamburg and was based around Germans 'salting' beef to preserve it, a process which had the by-product of also making the meat tough. So, in order to tenderise, they minced it and added spices and onion before grilling.

As the settlers flocked to America with the promise of a new life, salted beef was taken to feed families on the long sea journey from Germany – once in America, the recipe became known as Hamburger Style Steaks, soon proving hugely popular and spreading beyond New York from the 1850s.

These were the forerunner of today's hamburgers and explain why one of the staple ingredients for any BBQ – the burger - begins with the word 'ham' yet is normally made of beef.

WHEN IS A BURGER A HAMBURGER?
JUST ASK THE GOVERNOR OF OKLAHOMA

The debate over where the first hamburger came from has gone on for nearly as long as hamburgers themselves.

In 1995, Governor Keating got so irate at Texan claims to have invented the hamburger that he passed an official state proclamation to back up the long-staked claim of Oscar Weber Bilby, from Tulsa, Oklahoma. Back in 1891, the story goes, Bilby used his wife's yeast buns to house his hamburgers and the idea caught on at well-attended 4th of July parties. So much so, his family set up a stall in the 1930s to sell them.

"The first true hamburger on a bun, as meticulous research shows, was created and consumed in Tulsa in 1891 and was only copied for resale at the St. Louis World's Fair a full 13 years after that momentous and history-making occasion:

Now therefore, I, Frank Keating,
Governor of the State of Oklahoma, do hereby proclaim
April 12, 1995,
THE REAL BIRTHPLACE OF THE HAMBURGER IN TULSA."

Hence, the State of Oklahoma felt it had set the record straight once and for all.

As suggested though, Oklahoma is not the only place to lay claim to being the home of the hamburger. Just five years later a response to Oklahoma's claim came from the House of Representative in Connecticut where Rosa DeLauro stood up to announce her pleasure in observing the year 2000 as the 105th anniversary of the hamburger being created by Louis Lassen of New Haven, Connecticut.

The Louis' Lunch café he set up is still serving what it claims to be the original hamburger. The burgers are grilled vertically and served between toast. Don't ask for mustard or ketchup, though, they're banned!

...So far, the mayor of Hamburg has yet to join the debate.

Another widely acknowledged claim comes from Austin Texas, where a local café owner Fletcher Davis - known as 'Old Dave' – had been serving hamburger style steak sandwiches since the late 1800s. He took the idea of a fast food sandwich to the St Louis fair in 1904, it got reported in the New York Tribune and the idea caught on. However, it is possible that his hamburgers were placed between two slices of toast, rather than in a bun.

PERFECT BBQ PUBS

As much fun as it is to hold your own BBQ, there always comes a time when it's nice to let someone else do all of the work, leaving you to enjoy yourself with friends, which is why PIMM'S® has conducted a nationwide search for the best BBQ pubs in Britain.

Perfect sausages, a picturesque location, friendly staff...there are many factors that define what makes a great BBQ pub. The shortlist of the 100 top BBQ inns and public houses picks out some of the very best in Britain.

South West
Avon George Hotel, Bristol
Beachcomber, Burham on Sea, Somerset
Berryhead Hotel, Brixham
Brixham Yacht Club, Brixham
Buckle Grove Caravan Park, Rodney Stoke, Somerset
Delfter Krug, Bath

Dolphin Inn, Bath
The Exeter Inn, Bampton, North Devon
The Jolly Sailor, Saltford
The London Inn, Braunton, North Devon
Racks, Clifton
Riverside Inn, Cheddar, Somerset
The Tavern, Barnstable

Southern England
Beach House, Christchurch
Boathouse, Christchurch
Chequers, Lymington, Hampshire
Customs House, Poole
Fusion Inn, Lymington
Greyhound Inn, Wareham
Gordelton Mill Hotel, Hordle, Nr. Lymington
Haven Bistro, Yachthaven
Mayflower, Waterford
Rising Sun, Christchurch
Salisbury Arms, Christchurch
Salterns Hotel, Poole
Thomas Tripp, Christchurch
Thomas Tripp, Lymington

South East
The Bear, Brighton
Crooked Billet, Leigh-On-Sea
The Duke of Edinburgh, Ascot
Exchange, Hove
Grand Central, Brighton
The Hub, Brighton
Ollies, Ascot
Open House, Brighton
Percy Arms, Guilford
Polar East, Brighton
Shepherd and Flock, Farnham
The Sidewinder, Brighton
Wellington Arms, Berkshire
The Weyside, Guilford
Wheatsheaf, Worthing
Ye Old Red Lion, Oakley Green

London
Anglers, Teddington
Aragon House, New King's Road
Canonbury Tavern, Islington
Circle Bar, Clapham
Coe Vinter, Redbridge
Crown & Greyhound, Dulwich
Dovedale House, Battersea
Edinburgh Castle, Camden
The Falcon, Clapham
Ganleys, Herne Hill, SE London
The Grange, Ealing Common
The Greyhound, Kew
Henrys, Avely
Hope (Faith & Firkin), Wandsworth

The Imperial, King's Road
Jets, South Woodford
The Lion, Teddintgon
Metropolitan Police Sports Club, Chigwell
Morrison, King's Road
Narrow Street Pub & Dining Room, Limehouse, East London
New Inn, Ealing
Orsett Hall Hotel, Orsett
Royal Oak, Loughton
The Smoke Rooms, Clapham
Upminster Golf Club, Upminster
Doggetts Coat & Badge, Blackfriars
HMS President, Victoria Embankment
Hornimans at Hays, Tooley Street
Mudlark, London Bridge
Old Thameside Inn, Pickford's Wharf
Pub on the Park, Hackney
Royal Inn on the Park, Hackney

Midlands
Bear Inn, Oxford
Chequers Inn, Oxford
Coopers Arms, Weston-on-Trent, Derby
Crown, Oxford
The Goose, Selly Oak, Birmingham
The Goose, Oxford

North & Scotland
Black Bull, Yarm, Nr. Stockton on Tees
Charles XII, Heslington, York
The Durham Ox, Crayke, North Yorkshire
Duke of York, Grindleton, Lancashire
Hand & Dagger, Nr Preston
Oaks Golf Club, Aughton, York
Old Wellington, Manchester
Original Oak Inn, Headingley, Leeds
Royal Hotel, Nr. Carnforth, Lancashire
Sheep Heid Inn, Edinburgh
Three Hares, Bilborough, York
The Windmill, York

Wales
Eli Jenkins, Cardiff
Pen & Wig, Cardiff
Railway Hotel, Penarth
Talacre Beach Caravan & Leisure Park North Wales
White Rose, Mumbles, Swansea

"Chipolatas Tabitha - Oh! how charmingly post modern"

HINTS FOR THE PERFECT BBQ BURGERS

- Add a tablespoon of (olive) oil per pound of beef to keep the mix moist and help it bind
- Coarser minced beef will hold moisture better
- Splash water on hands before mixing, it keeps the ingredients moist and stops them sticking to you
- Add a cup of tomato juice to the mixture to keep it moist and add flavour
- Lightly mix the ingredients; if you over mix, your burgers will be too dense

SPARE RIBS A PLENTY

American meals are renowned for generous portions but, it seems, John DeMarco from California took the reputation for big eating to an extreme when he spit roasted seven buffaloes in 1973.

The feat still holds the Guinness World Record for the largest ever spit roast. The buffaloes weighed in at a cumulative 1,703kg (3,775lb) and took 26 hours to cook over a 12ft long pit.

BANGERS ARE NOT THE ONLY PORK

It may be the most common ingredient in sausages but there's far more to pork than simply bangers.

Certainly Faye and David Chadwick, who run Piggybank Farm (www.piggybank-farm.co.uk) in Kent, believe that although people often think of it as a dry meat, get the right pork and cook it well, and it is fantastic for barbecuing. They allow their British rare breed pigs (Tamworths and Middle Whites) to forage in natural woodland and to mature naturally and suggest this healthy approach gives the best results for BBQs.

"If you allow a rare breed pig to feed and mature naturally, you get the tastiest pork because it has fat spread through it, and it's the fat that gives the texture and flavour," insists Faye.

For the grill, she suggests asking a butcher for bacon steaks as well as pork chops. The former come from the rear of the pig, where the tastiest, most tender meat is whereas chops come from along the back bone.

In case you were wondering, the difference between pork, bacon and ham is that bacon and ham have been cured, pork has not. Curing involves standing the meat in salted water to draw moisture from it so it is preserved. The tradition has come about because while a farmer would normally eat, say, a chicken all at once, a pig provides much more meat and so needs to be preserved for the months ahead. After curing, the meat can be smoked to add flavour.

PICKING OUT AND COOKING PORK

When asking a quality butcher for a bacon steak or chops, Faye's main piece of advice is to look at its colour.

"You want to avoid white, pale meat," she advises, "our meat has some colour to it, it's pinker because it's got some fat in it that will give flavour and keep the meat moist."

This is crucial with pork because it is a meat that many people associate with being tasteless and overcooked. Hence, once you've chosen pink bacon steak or pork chops for the grill, the main thing is not to let the moisture be completely lost.

"People cook pork at too high a temperature and then wonder why it's dry," Faye suggests, "we do hog roasts for parties and we would generally cook a whole pig on the spit overnight, the bare minimum would be six to eight hours. So with pork or bacon steaks, the key is to cook them slowly on the BBQ."

BASTING SAUCE

If you are worried about pork drying out, brushing a basting sauce on the meat as it cooks is a good idea. This involves brushing on a mixture to add taste and moistness before the meat goes on the grill as well as while it's cooking.

There are many recipes available, but this is a good starting point – it is designed for 10 or 12 pork chops, so you may need to reduce quantities accordingly for just a handful of chops.

950ml of Cider Vinegar	*50g brown sugar*	*3 tbsp salt*
1 tbsp red pepper flakes	*1 tsp cayenne pepper*	*1 tsp ground black pepper*

HOW TO HOLD A SAFE BBQ

The Fire Service's top tips for a safe BBQ include:

- Always site a BBQ on level ground
- Make sure it is sited away from overhanging trees or sheds
- Never use petrol or let a BBQ burn wildly
- Do not wear loose trailing clothing and tie back hair
- Always have a bucket of water handy
- Never let children play near the BBQ
- Let embers cool before throwing away – use the bucket of water if in doubt

For outdoor gas cookers the Fire Service also recommends:

- Check tubes for splits, nicks or blockage and fix if necessary
- Fix worn connectors
- Move the gas bottle and hoses so they are not next to heat
- Never smoke or have a naked flame around a gas BBQ
- Store gas bottles upright, away from heat
- Again, if the flames are low DON'T THROW ON PETROL

THE GENDER DIVIDE
WHO'S MORE ACCIDENT PRONE?

The UK government commissioned a team of scientists to plot injuries throughout the '90s.

The government's researchers found that compared to women, British men are a hazard to themselves, with men accounting for 69% of all accidents; this leaves women responsible for a 31% share.

To put that into perspective, the DTI compared UK figures with the US where there is a 57%-43% ratio between men and women injuring themselves at the BBQ.

The researchers put the difference down to British men being more preoccupied with always being the chef at their own BBQ, whereas in America cooking duties are more likely to be shared.

However, Britons, even British men, can take solace that they are still considerably safer than Americans who have three times as many accidents per capita as the UK.

"Bob works in health and safety"

BIG BUCKS BURGERS

We all wonder what we get for the money by upgrading from economy to premium burgers but renowned chef Daniel Boulud went a whole stage further for the opening of his DB Bistro Moderne in New York.

In January 2003, he put the world's first $50 (£27) burger on the menu to make sure he could claim, by nearly $10, to have the most expensive burger in town.

The DB Burger Royale is offered in black truffle season (December to March) and consists of a ground sirloin steak with a filling of ribs braised in red wine, foie gras and black truffles.

The finishing touch comes from a bun made to a special recipe, including parmesan and poppy seeds, and comes coated with fresh horseradish, tomato confit, fresh tomato, red onion and lettuce.

The DB Burger Royale clearly proved a hit, as two years after launch it was selling for $69 (£37) – with pommes frites thrown in, of course.

The DB Burger (without truffles) sells year round for just $29.

GREENS SUPREME

When Guy Watson, an organic vegetable farmer based near Riverford in South Devon, (www.riverford.co.uk) throws a BBQ his favourite dish is the simplest to prepare.

As he lights the coals, the nearby safety bucket of water comes into its own as he throws in a bunch of sweetcorns, still in their husks.

"You need it to soak up lots of water but you keep the husks on because it protects the sweetcorn as it's cooking," says Guy. After soaking in water, just place them on the grill to cook.

"You can tell when a couple of the segments start to get a little charred that they're ready to eat, then the trick is to peel back the husk for your guests to hold on to while eating. Just let them cool a little first!"

"Sweetcorn not only looks and tastes great, it even comes with its own handle for BBQ guests!"

After that, Guy's favourite simple BBQ tip is to slice courgettes in half and then brush with olive oil. Add a pinch of rosemary, salt and pepper and he claims there is nothing tastier you can put on the grill:

"Courgettes are one of those fabulous vegetables that taste great barbecued," he points out, "The real trick is to get them on the day they've been picked or as soon after as possible, so it pays to shop with local producers. If you put a courgette in a cold room for a week or so, as can sometimes happen, you'll lose a lot of the taste."

Of course, no BBQ would be complete without vegetable kebabs and so Guy suggests adding pepper, courgette, mushroom and onion slices on skewers after they've been marinated overnight.

BIG IS BEAUTIFUL

If room is looking a little tight on your BBQ grill count yourself lucky you didn't ask J J Tranfield from Sheffield to make the sausages. To set a Guinness World Record in 2000, on behalf of a supermarket chain, he made a sausage nearly 60km long (that's nearly 37 miles).

The feat almost dwarves the World's largest Hot Dog which was made by a bunch of extremely busy students from the University of Pretoria in 2003 and measured 10.5m (34ft).

Not to be outdone though, Loran Green from Montana, USA still holds the Guinness World Record for largest burger. In 1999 her massive burger weighed in at 2,740kg (6,040lb) and measured 7.32m (24ft) across.

"A tale without love is like beef without mustard, an insipid dish."

ANATOLE FRANCE

JOHN TORODE'S
BBQ PRAWNS IN COCONUT MILK WITH RED CURRY PASTE

SERVES 10 WITH A FEW EXTRAS FOR THE GREEDY GUTS

I love prawns on the barbie, I grew up with them and I still think that large prawns cooked over charcoal and then peeled and eaten while still warm is one of the best food stuffs in the world. The coconut and the red curry paste give a sweet and spicy edge and I still love that crunch when you sink your teeth into a fresh barbecued king prawn.

You will need 12 bamboo skewers, one small mixing bowl, and a small pot. Pre-heat the BBQ and have it ready to go.

1 tsp of red curry paste
2 tsp of sugar
1 tbsp of vegetable oil

1 tin of coconut milk
12 large prawns de-veined and shelled
12 bamboo skewers

In a small pot or pan heat the oil and fry off the red curry paste, fry well until starting to go fragrant. Add the sugar and reduce the heat by half, stir the sugar in well until it dissolves, starts to bubble and is almost caramelized. Add the coconut milk, stir well and increase the heat, bring the coconut milk to the boil and reduce it by half.

In the meantime thread the prawns onto the wooden skewers and set to one side. When the coconut milk is boiled and reduced, remove from the heat, stir and leave to cool for five minutes. Pour the curry coconut milk over the top of the prawn and leave to sit for ten minutes. Place the prawns onto the BBQ and cook for approximately four to five minutes on each side until the prawns turn nice and pink. Serve as they are.

An extra tip

When barbecuing with wooden skewers firstly soak them in water for an hour before you thread them with the food. This does two things; the water stops any splinters; and they will be nice and damp and therefore will not burn over the flames of the BBQ.

SPRING INTO BBQ SEASON
WITH LAMB

An old saying that is particularly true of BBQs is that, according to organic, rare-breed sheep farmer Jane Kallaway from Wiltshire, you really can't dress mutton up as lamb.

"Lamb's probably only around six months old and so it's a lot more tender and moist than mutton," she says, "as you can lose a lot of moisture on the BBQ grill if you're not careful, it really is best to start off with the most tender meat in the first place."

Jane Kallaway farms Manx Loghtan sheep near Chippenham in Wiltshire (www.langleychase.co.uk). The breed is ancient, and now rare, and was reared by Iron Age man, particularly in the Islands off the British coast, hence the Manx name.

Whilst Jane suggests there is nothing wrong with mass sheep farming, she does recommend those seeking out the best quality meat to ask their butcher for rare breed, locally-sourced lamb. This will almost certainly be darker than mass-produced lamb and is likely to have a little more fat covering. Her Manx Loghtan meat, for example, was singled out by Mark Hix, Chief Director at top London restaurants The Ivy and Le Caprice for its unusual 'gamey' taste.

When it comes to picking cuts of lamb, Jane's suggestion is shoulder for kebabs, because it cuts well into cubes for skewering, whilst legs of lamb give the best results on the BBQ. They have just the right combination of fat and meat to give flavour and moisture while providing a large piece of meat for guests to cut into.

To ensure they have as much flavour as possible Jane – a cooking fan who loves barbecuing in the summer – advises smearing leg steaks, or kebabs, with mint jelly, then sprinkling on some crushed, dried chillies before 'drizzling' the meat with olive oil (or garlic olive oil). This not only gives a lovely flavour but it also keeps the meat moist as well as making it smell 'fantastic' as it's cooking on the grill.

In fact, to aid the smell, as well as the taste, Jane often pats a couple of tablespoons of chopped rosemary on to lamb legs cooking on her BBQ.

"The rosemary tastes fantastic but it also falls into the coals and I can assure you there is no better smell to get people ready for their lunch or dinner than lamb and rosemary," she enthuses.

Always one keen to promote chefs to experiment with their lamb, she advises those starting out to try a simple baste mixture which they can put on the meat before it goes on the grill and then brush on as it's cooking to make sure it doesn't dry out.

UK SAUSAGE MAP

Scottish

Cumberland

Lorne

Tomato

Lincolnshire

Beer

Suffolk

Lamb

Pork and leek

Glamorgan

Gloucester

Oxford

Marylebone

══════ POPULAR VARIETIES OF UK SAUSAGE ══════

Beer . . . . .Normally ale is added to pork sausages, sometimes GUINNESS® is added to beef

Cumberland . . . . .Known as the 'meatiest' sausage in the UK. It is made in spirals and spiced with pepper

Glamorgan . . . . .One for the vegetarians, made from Caerphilly cheese, spring onions, eggs and herbs. As it's skinless, it's not technically a sausage, but it tastes good so who cares?

Gloucester . . . . .Traditionally from the Gloucester Old Spot pig and seasoned with sage

Lamb . . . . .Popular in Wales, and normally flavoured with leek, mint or rosemary

Lincolnshire . . . . .Traditional pork sausage with bread and sage (sometimes thyme)

Lorne . . . . .This square beef or pork sausage is smooth in texture and native to Scotland

Marylebone . . . . .Traditional London sausage with pork, ginger, mace and sage

Oxford . . . . .Pork, veal and lemon with sage and marjoram herbs

Pork and leek . . . . .Popular in Wales, often seasoned with ginger

Scottish . . . . .Tends to be made with beef and a finer paté like consistency

Suffolk . . . . .Similar to Lincolnshire, often coarser in texture

Tomato . . . . .Pork with 10% tomato gives a red colour, often mixed with basil. Most popular in the Midlands

Venison . . . . .Often mixed with pork with red wine, garlic and juniper berries

Wild boar . . . . .Darker and stronger than pork sausages, often with apples, red wine or garlic

LONG AND MOIST, THAT'S THE KEY

A pan of water is normally the sort of accessory you would only imagine at a BBQ as a safety precaution, however, chef Paul reveals it is the key to succulent meat:

"I place the hot coals on one side of the grill and then have a pan of water next to them at the same level,"
he says, "that way the water will simmer for hours and keep the atmosphere around it moist. I keep the lid on
the pan but you still get enough moisture to stop the meat drying out."

Paul also only cooks at around 230-250 Fahrenheit, which is relatively low for a BBQ. This way he can cook meat over a long period so it remains moist and evenly cooked.

Paul will cook brisket for 14-16 hours to make it tender while ribs normally take five to six hours and chicken around four hours. Perhaps this is one reason why the Champ isn't from these shores, where we'd have to take a bit of a gamble with the great British weather to cook al fresco for 14 hours!

THE WORLD IS JUST A GREAT BIG ONION

Paul Kirk's BBQ secrets aren't limited to meat. In fact, one of his World Championship winning meals was vegetarian. His 'Onion Mum' is a great main meal or accompaniment. It is an onion barbecued in teriyaki sauce, which he assures is easy to make.

Onion Mum: *235ml of pineapple juice*   *235ml of soy sauce*   *115g of sugar*
 1 tsp ground garlic   *1 tsp ground ginger*

Add these to a pan and bring to the simmer. At the same time mix in a bowl

 2 tbsp of cornflour   *3 tbsp of cold water*

Add the above to the simmering liquid in the pan so it thickens and stir for a couple of minutes.

Next, take a large onion and make eight incisions from the top down but do not cut in to the core. Then place it in foil and pour in the teriyaki sauce.

Cook on the BBQ for around five minutes and when it is unwrapped the onion will have opened up like the Chrysanthemum flower, hence the name of the dish.

Paul suggests serving to decorate a fresh salad, making it even more appealing to the eye with slices of different colour peppers.

TOP TEN SONGS TO ENJOY AT A BBQ

Smoke Gets In Your Eyes . . . . .The Platters
Light My Fire . . . . .The Doors
Jumpin' Jack Flash (It's a Gas! Gas! Gas!) . . . . .Rolling Stones
(You Always Take The) Weather With You .Crowded House
We Didn't Start The Fire . . . . .Billy Joel
Summertime . . . . The Fresh Prince
(Burn Baby, Burn) Disco Inferno . . . . .The Trammps
Here Comes The Sun . . . . .The Beatles
Roll With It . . . . .Oasis
The Ketchup Song . . . . .Las Ketchup

BEEF IS BEST SUNNY SIDE UP

The sun doesn't only tell you when it's a good time to get the coals burning on the BBQ, it also illuminates where the best cuts of beef come from.

That's the advice from Carolyn Fletcher who rears Aberdeen Angus beef cattle in Cumbria. If you want to know which cuts will give guests the most tender steaks, just imagine where the sun would reach first if a cow were grazing in a field.

"The tenderest meat comes from muscle that isn't used," she explains, "so that means all along the top of the ribs, down the back and to the rump. As soon as you go lower into the shade, you're on the legs and they obviously do a lot of work holding up a heavy animal, so they're less tender."

Hence ribs, rib-eye, fillet and rump are the most tender and tasty cuts to put on the BBQ, with Carolyn normally suggesting al fresco chefs go for rump because it is less expensive than other 'top side' steaks but is still full of flavour.

The cut of meat, though, is only part of the equation. While it can be easy to just think of beef as any other meat, Carolyn insists that those in charge of the BBQ should do their homework on where the beef is coming from.

"I breed pure-bred Aberdeen Angus because they provide the tastiest meat and they've got a lovely temperament," she reveals, "I'd advise buyers to always stick with the natural British breeds because they're raised on grass which makes them far tastier than continental breeds that eat grain and are then 'finished' on barley.

"It gives their meat a far coarser, more fibrous texture. So, always look out for breeds such as the Aberdeen Angus, Highland, Hereford and Galloway because it's far more natural to eat meat raised on grass and it also means they've had a good life grazing in open fields for as long as possible."

So, in her opinion, picking the right type of cattle is even more important than the actual cut of meat.

"If someone's throwing a BBQ and they want the best quality meat, I'd advise they go to a quality butcher and ask them what breed of cattle the meat's come from, has it been produced locally and how has it been hung? Ideally you want a good British breed that's been reared locally on grass and hung for three weeks.

"My meat is a far darker red than the brighter red cuts you see in many shops and it is almost marbled by tiny lines of fat. These melt away as the meat is cooked and add flavour as well as keep a steak moist, which is really crucial if you're barbecuing them."

So, Carolyn's advice is to make sure the steaks that are going on the grill are a dark, dull red and have tiny streaks of fat. That way, not only will you have the best quality meat possible, it will retain its taste and moisture better than an inferior steak.

With barbecuing her most important piece of advice is not to go to the lengths of sourcing quality meat only to 'incinerate' it over the coals.

"Make sure the coals are really hot and sear both sides by turning from one side to the other when it first goes on the grill," she advises, "then grill each side until they're browned. The worst thing you can do is cook the beef for too long because you lose all the flavour. The key is to make sure it is still pink in the middle and that if you cut into it, the fluid is still pinkish. If it's clear, you've ruined the meat.

"I know people are worried about anything coming off the grill pink, but as long as the meat is properly produced and fresh there's nothing to worry about."

"Beef is the soul of cooking."

MARIE-ANTOINE CARSME

BEEF CUTS

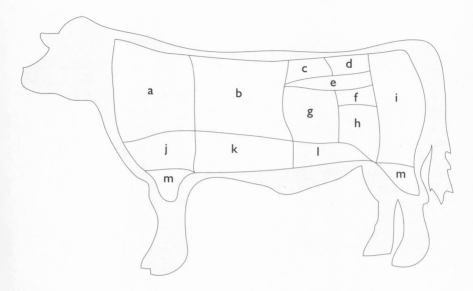

KEY:

a . . . . .CHUCK
b . . . . .RIB
c . . . . .SHORT LOIN
d . . . . .SIRLOIN
e . . . . .TENDERLOIN
f . . . . .TOP SIRLOIN
g . . . . .SHORT LOIN
h . . . . .BOTTOM SIRLOIN
i . . . . .ROUND
. . . . .BRISKET
k . . . . .PLATE
. . . . .FLANK
m . . . . .SHANK

"Any of us would kill a cow, rather than not have beef."

SAMUEL JOHNSON

JOHN TORODE'S
MARINATED LAMB IN YOGHURT AND THYME
WITH CUCUMBER AND MINT

SERVES 10

Lamb rump steaks are now available in good supermarkets as well as butchers but you can also use this recipe for lamb cutlets. Be generous with the lemon juice and the yoghurt as it will make it taste that much better. I have found over the years that I prefer naan bread as bought from a supermarket to pitta bread, however you can also use tortillas, or my favourite - Greek flat bread which I buy from a local Greek deli.

400ml Plain Yoghurt (Greek is good)
2 lemons juiced
8 x 250g pieces of lamb
12 flat breads
2 large cucumbers
1 tsp salt
1 tsp garam marsala
Salt and pepper

First pre-heat the BBQ.

Take the eight pieces of lamb and place them in the large bowl; sprinkle liberally with salt and pepper and add $^3/_4$ of the lemon juice. Stir well and leave to sit for ten minutes.

Peel the cucumber, halve lengthways and remove the seeds. Cut the cucumber into decent slices and mix with the remaining lemon juice and $^1/_4$ of the yoghurt, add the garam marsala and the salt and mix well.

Pour the remaining yoghurt over the lamb and mix well. Take the lamb and place it on the BBQ, cook for five minutes and then turn - the edges and the outer should be quite dark as the yoghurt cooks. Cook for a further five minutes and then repeat. The process should take about 20 minutes, but the lamb could be cooked a little longer if you wish. Place on a board and cut into thick bite size pieces.

Take the flat bread and heat over the BBQ or on the grill, spoon on some cucumbe mix and top with the barbecued lamb and any juice that is left on the board.

Season and serve.

═════ BARBECUES, JACK, TREVOR AND ME ═════
MAUREEN LIPMAN

"Make a barbecue and griddle out of your own hob!" screamed a Woolworth's' sales promotional today. I was out buying paper plates, which is as near as I get to entertaining these days. I compensate by being a wonderful guest. Flowers, thank you notes, chocolates, punctuality, hilarious self-deprecating anecdotes - I'm yer man. Roasting a side of lamb in the open air with a choice of marinades, a plethora of salads, perfectly cooked sausages and spuds - may I direct you in the direction of my friend, Trevor?

Now Trevor can really barbecue. He has an M.A. in marinading and a PhD in barbecuing. I would cross a barren desert on a kebab skewer for one of Trevor's barbecues. Without barbs, I would queue, for just one of his sizzling sausages. Even my late husband, Jack, who couldn't really understand the principle of barbecues, when you've got a perfectly usable oven which requires no rubbing together of incendiary devices, would happily put on a sweater to sit outside chez-Trev and sample his host's, sizzling saussisons and sirloins. (I know. I'm a sub-editor's secret fantasy).

"This meat is unbelievably tender", Jack would moan, teeth covered in mustard but not caring a granule. "It's like butter! I mean, there's none of that black charcoal-y stuff either! How do you do it?"

Trevor would adjust his professional chef's apron, smile his professorial smile, prod and turn another tenderloin and say "It's all in the meat. Good meat - good barbecue."

I personally have nothing against a nice if slightly lukewarm meal al fresco, as t'were, give or take a cloudburst or three. For years we had a gregarious and lively Greek family living next door to us. With the first daffodils came the first trail of smoke over the fence. The smell was intoxicating, likewise the sound of Greek music and conversation. We were often invited to join in and it was a convivial and delicious way of passing an afternoon.

Jack wasn't keen on eating outdoors. He didn't really understand the concept. In his northern childhood you played outdoors all day - ran in for your food, then ran out again to smash your leather football bladder against the alley wall 'til the sun dropped behind the factory chimney and a clip over the ear brought you tenderly to bed. (Cue ukelele music.) Even the idea of a picnic disturbed him. He was uncomfortable on the grass and finicky over the menu. Nothing fancy. Pesto goats cheese - nil points. Egg and cress sandwiches, with the crusts off - dix poi

I did buy a barbecue and a pair of tongs in John Lewis once. It was one of th black cauldron jobs on legs, which made me want to hum "Danse Macabre", attempted to wheel it over the uneven patio. We waited for a day we were all hc at once and the sky wasn't lowering, invited a few mates and lit the thing. Then waited for it to achieve combustibility and then Jack poked and prodded ultimately achieved the kind of meat he resolutely refused to eat. I put the lid b on it and wheeled it off stage left.

I haven't entirely given up though. Vegetable kebabs are what I'm hankering at Lovely courgettes and aubergines and peppers of many colours, left to marinat honey and mustard or soy sauce for as long as Delia tells me to, then slung on barbie to seal in their succulence.

In short, I probably won't be picked for a reality TV show called "It's Your BAR! CUE!" hosted by Nicky Clarke and Steve Davis. I've only really just mastered oven. After years of believing that EVERYONE'S oven took two hours to bak potato, I'm flabbergasted to find I can cook one in 30 minutes. In between purch and realisation there have been an awful lot of well-charred meals. So it may pointless to ask me to contribute to this important book...thanks for as! though...and would you like TREVOR'S NUMBER?

Maureen Lipman

WHAT'S GOOD FORM AT A BBQ?

Most of us have a basic knowledge of what constitutes good and bad form around the dining table. But how far do guidelines that have evolved over centuries of formal parties extend to the comparatively new passion for BBQs?

Everyone knows that BBQs are informal, relaxed affairs and so nobody is going to be blackballed for passing PIMM'S® to the right; but what rules can one discard as dinner parties move from the dining room to the garden?

The traditional bible for good manners, Debretts, does not cover al fresco eating in any great depth, leaving social butterflies to wonder whether invites should still be accepted in the third person and, if cancelling first on the phone and then confirming in writing is still 'the done thing'.

Thankfully, though, a Swiss finishing school has been teaching young ladies in the making, as well as businessmen and women, the finer art of impeccable manners at BBQs for the past ten years.

In the mountains overlooking Lake Geneva the Surval Mont-Fleuri finishing school (www.surval.ch) devotes an entire module to letting its clients know how to be the perfect host or guest at a BBQ. The school has been quick to realise the growing popularity of al fresco dining raises many questions as to how much guests can relax without appearing ill-mannered.

According to Philippe Neri, the school's Director, those concerned about manners need not fret because BBQs, even in the highest social echelons, are regarded as relaxed affairs. As such, dress code is definitely casual and guests should only bear a few pointers in mind.

"The really obvious thing to watch is that you don't pile up food," he explains, "You should take a little of whatever you like but make sure it doesn't overtake the plate, that really isn't very good manners."

While we all probably have a good idea who could benefit from that particular piece of advice, everyone can rest assured that a BBQ is a relaxed enough affair to confirm attendance on the phone – no real need for a formal note on headed paper, Philippe advises. However, where one does have to be a little careful is the dreaded question of 'what should I bring'?

Just as you wouldn't normally bring round a lamp chop if attending a roast dinner at a friend's house, Philippe suggests that taking food is not good form.

"It's just the same as with a dinner invitation, never arrive with food," he explains, "you should take a very nice wine but it should be a gift bottle. It's not for the host to open that night, it's for them to enjoy as a gift from you at a later date." Or perhaps even a bottle of PIMM'S® is ideal on a hot summer's day.

Flowers are a possibility but the same rule that applies to dinner should be borne in mind – a good guest never arrives with a bouquet because it leaves a busy hostess with her hands full looking for a vase. Instead the well-mannered guest should either send flowers in advance, or as Philippe Neri suggests, send them the next day.

Etiquette issues do not just apply to guests, of course. All hosts should make sure they have checked in advance if people have special dietary requirements. This is not only to make sure vegetarians are well catered for but to ensure that religious considerations are met – pork and beef rubbing against one another on the same grill could raise dietary problems for anyone keeping kosher for example.

The main thing, for comfort when eating, is for the hosts to provide plates with clip-on holders for drinks and, if cooking food that needs to be eaten with a knife and fork, ensure that sufficient cutlery is made available. Sufficient seating should also be offered so guests are not left trying to cut a steak with a dessert spoon without spilling their glass of PIMM'S®.

In the main, Philippe Neri assures, hosts and guests need not get too anxious about 'form' at BBQs because they are casual, outdoor events where common sense and everyday courtesy are the order of the day.

"One of the delights of life is eating with friends, second to that is talking about eating. And, for an unsurpassed double whammy, there is talking about eating while you are eating with friends."

LAURIE COLWIN

STARTER LAMB BASTE

4oz butter
4 tbsp grated orange peel, chopped parsley and mint
2 tbsp organic honey
Juice half a lemon or balsamic vinegar
Splash of fresh orange juice (to taste)

GETTING PLUMMY WITH LEG STEAKS

This is Jane's favourite marinade which she uses to soak lamb before it goes on the BBQ as well as a baste while it is cooking. She then also offers it to guests as an accompanying sauce.

500g red plums, quartered and stoned
250ml sweet cider
1 knob butter
1 medium red onion diced
2 tbsp brown sugar
1 tbsp balsamic vinegar
1 tsp ground or minced ginger

Melt the butter in a saucepan and cook the onion until transparent and slightly browning. Add the cider and plums, brown sugar, vinegar and ginger and cook until the plums are soft and mushy.

BEAR FACED CHEEK

A group of Canadian hunters had a lucky escape when they sat down to a BBQ in the Rockies. The smell of the cooking food attracted a family of Grizzly bears, one of whom sat on their jeep, which had their guns inside, while the others tucked in to what the hunters had hoped would be their dinner.

Terrified and rooted to the spot, the hunters believe they only survived because one of the bears trod on the burning charcoal and fled, prompting the family to follow.

HAVE A WORLD-CLASS BBQ

If you're determined to make your BBQ the best of the summer, who better to turn to for advice than twice World BBQ Champion, Paul Kirk, from Kansas City.

Such is Paul Kirk's devotion to improving the standard of BBQs that he has now set up his own BBQ Cookery Course to help anyone from an aspiring chef to a back garden fire worshipper to improve their al fresco cooking.

His main observation on why barbecued meat can seem a little drier than normal and sometimes lacking in taste is that most chefs are not truly barbecuing - and they're not doing it for long enough. While most of us do little more than slap a steak or couple of chops on for a few minutes, he suggests this is just 'grilling' - not barbecuing.

If you want to start winning world championships, you need to cook your meat more slowly, and in a moist atmosphere. That means a pan of water, a low temperature and a cooking time of at least five hours!

Keeping a written record of every BBQ you make is vital, insists our World Champion, because it's the only way you can go back to your notes and learn from mistakes and successes alike.

RUBBING IT UP THE RIGHT WAY

The first thing you'll need to do according to Paul is to get your 'rub' right. Rub is a sugar and salt mix that no World Champion worth his, erm, salt would be without.

The rub not only adds flavour to meat it also helps coat it to retain moisture. The mix should be applied before it is cooked and can also be added while it is cooking.

Recipes vary but Paul Kirk suggests the following.

225g of white cane sugar (not brown, as it can go clumpy)
225g made up evenly with salt, garlic, celery and onion (all finely chopped)
115g paprika
2 tbsp oregano
2 tbsp black pepper
Chilli powder to taste
1 tbsp of your favourite three spices (e.g. cayenne pepper, cumin and ground ginger)

"Eat with the fingers, drink with the nose."

JOSEPH DELTEIL

"A highbrow is the kind of person who looks at a sausage and thinks of Picasso."

SIR ALAN PATRICK HERBERT

"Be careful not to be the first to put your hands in the dish. What you cannot hold in your hands you must put on your plate. Also it is a great breach of etiquette when your fingers are dirty and greasy, to bring them to your mouth in order to lick them, or to clean them on your jacket. It would be more decent to use the tablecloth."

DESIDERIUS ERASMUS

"Never eat more than you can lift."

MISS PIGGY